Savannah Monitor Lizards as Pets

The Ultimate Guide for Savannah Monitors

General Info, Purchasing, Care, Cost, Keeping, Health, Supplies, Food, Breeding and More Included!

By Lolly Brown

Copyrights and Trademarks

Disclaimer and Legal Notice

Foreword

Savannah monitors are commonly found in the savannahs of Central Africa extending to the sub – Saharan Africa particularly in eastern Senegal, Sudan and also the southern area of the Congo River as well as the Rift Valley. They grow relatively large and even if they are gentle animals, you should keep in mind that these are still very powerful creatures and will require a serious keeper. In this book, you'll learn everything about Savannah monitors including its breed, behavior, general information, biological background, origin and distribution, how to maintain it, and also keep it healthy. This book will also delve deeper on how to take care of Savannah monitors in terms of feeding, breeding, habitat requirements as well as its licensing process.

Table of Contents

Introduction

About 65 million years ago, a cataclysm wipe out the ruling reptiles which are the dinosaurs but only monitor lizards survive. Of the nearly 5,000 types of lizards found today, the monitor lizards are the undisputed kings! Monitor lizards cannot regulate its body temperature internally but that doesn't mean they're sluggish, these creatures have the stamina, speed and intelligence of mammals.

Savannah monitor lizards unlike other species became popular as pets because of its relatively small size, cheap cost and because they have a docile disposition. These species can easily be handled and can be tamed compared to other aggressive and sometimes even poisonous monitor lizards.

In the next few chapters, you'll learn some general information, and biological background as well as the temperament of Savannah monitors lizards. This book will also delve deeper on how to maintain and keep monitors in terms of its health, nutrition, breeding and habitat. You will also learn how to properly handle them so that they can get used to being touched and not become afraid or aggressive towards people. Their own physical characteristics as well as its behaviors in the wild and in captivity will also be discussed. The information you'll get to learn in the next few chapters can help you better understand Savannah monitor lizards and their unique biological background.

Many first time keepers and experts in monitor lizards enjoy caring for savannah monitors because even if they look like real predators on the outside, these animals are longing to be petted by their owners on the inside as long as you treat them right and feed them well!

Chapter One: Biological Information

Savannah monitors are considered as one of the most docile monitor lizards in the world which is why they are perfect as pets. They grow relatively large and even if they are gentle animals, you should keep in mind that these are still very powerful creatures and will require a serious keeper. The question is, are you sure you're ready to deal and take care of these kinds of species? Let's find out! In this chapter you will receive an introduction to the Savannah monitor breed including some basic biological facts and general information about its sub – species. Find out if you think you can handle this lizards based on its physical traits and check out its sub – species to see which type best resonates with you.

Taxonomy, Origin and Distribution

Savannah monitors have a scientific name of *Varanus exanthematicus*. They belong in Kingdom *Animalia*, Phylum *Chordata*, Class *Reptilia*, Order *Squamata*, Family *Varanidae* Genus *Varanus*, and Species *V. exanthematicus*.

It might be quite obvious where these creatures got their name – yes from savannahs! Savannah monitors are commonly found in the savannahs of Central Africa extending to the sub – Saharan Africa particularly in eastern Senegal, Sudan and also the southern area of the Congo River as well as the Rift Valley. Even though these animals prefers living in savannahs in the wild, they also have adapted to living in rocky desserts, forests as well as woodlands, the places where you can't find them is deserts and also rainforests.

Savannah monitors have powerful jaws and sharp teeth that could crush the shell covering of snails or scorpions. They are carnivorous but mostly insectivores, in the wild they love to eat worms, eggs, smaller snakes, other smaller mammals, crickets, beetles, roaches and other types of insects.

These monitor lizards particularly the male species loves to fight with other savannah male monitors because they are very territorial. These creatures are mostly active during the day, and when they are threatened by their predators they defend themselves by lashing their tails or hissing loudly to scare off the potential predator. They are mostly terrestrial but they can also climb trees to hunt for food, reproduce or to also protect themselves against predators.

Most monitor lizards are quite defensive and aggressive in the wild but savannah monitors in general are easier to handle and they are much gentler than most lizards. Captive – bred savannah monitor lizards are very easy to tame and can also be trained for socialization, they also grow quite large which is perfect for handling if you really prefer bigger types of lizard species.

Size, Life Span, and Physical Appearance

Savannah monitors can reach to a length of about 4 ½ feet; females and hatchlings are mostly smaller in size. They are quite stout, have short limbs and toes but like most lizards, they have sharp and very strong claws use for climbing or digging. They weigh an average of 60 - 70 kg or about 150 pounds once they reach maturity. Savannah monitors also have forked tongues which make them the only lizard species to possess this physical trait because forked tongues are mostly found in snake species. They use it to accurately spot their prey's scent and also detect chemicals around them. They also possess a banded tail that is also very strong, and have bellies that come in a variety of colors. The savannah's head is mostly rectangular in shape and also flat, they have hundreds of small yet very sharp teeth and their skin is thick with approximately 60 to 100+ scales that are flat but has some pebble type of texture in it or keeled scales. Their colors range from gray to brown, the back part of their bodies has darkish yellow spots, and their tails have yellow or sometimes brown rings. Their tongues are blue in color like most snake species.

Like most reptiles, savannah monitors are heterothermic animals and have an average lifespan of 15 to 20 years. Most monitor lizards including savannah monitors are smart and powerful, but what makes them popular as pets is primarily because they are easy to handle and feed, quite playful and are also sweet animals if you socialize them at a young age.

Quick Facts

Distribution and Range: Western and Eastern Africa

Breed Size: stout and relatively large breed

Body Type and Appearance: Has flat head, stout body and around one hundred keel scales. The limbs are short and the claws are sharp; has very sharp teeth with a powerful jaw, forked tongue, tapered or banded tail.

Length: Savannah monitors can reach to a length of about 4 ½ feet; females and hatchlings are usually smaller in size.

Weight: They weigh an average of 60 - 70 kg or about 150 pounds once they reach maturity.

Skin Texture: scaly or has keeled scales

Color: Their colors range from gray to brown, the back part of their bodies has darkish yellow spots, and their tails have yellow or sometimes brown rings.

Temperament: docile, smart, easy to handle and tame, and also non – venomous.

Diet: In captivity they eat roaches, crickets, meal worms, wax worms, thawed mice; in the wild they eat other reptiles like snakes, bird's eggs, rodents and other smaller mammals.

Habitat: Savannahs, Woodlands and Grasslands

Health Conditions: generally healthy but predisposed to common illnesses such as intestinal parasites, metabolic bone disease, fatty liver disease, bacterial pneumonia

Lifespan: average 15 to 20 years

Chapter Two: Savannah Monitors as Pets

Now that you have a basic idea about what Savannah monitors are all about, and have a background knowledge about its different types, it's time to get to determine what makes this docile 'beasts' great pets or popular lizards. We will delve deeper on what it takes to really become a keeper by learning about its temperament as well as the license or permit needed for keeping them, and also the budget you'll most probably need to provide all its requirements. These are all important before you purchase a Savannah monitor lizard. Taking care of these large creatures needs total commitment.

Behavioral Characteristics and Interaction

As mentioned earlier, in the wild as well as in captivity, male savannah monitors tends to be aggressive in protecting their territories against other lizards or animals. Males usually make threats to intimidate or scare off other species, and usually if the trespasser is also another kind of monitor lizard, it will end up in a fight or a wrestling match which could cause severe injuries and sometimes fatality. This kind of territoriality behavior is still present among male savannah monitors that are captive – bred even if they have been living with another (male) species and has been properly socialize. But of course, don't be surprise if you see two males wrestling from time to time, it's their nature to do that.

They can feel if they are being threatened through their forked tongues. It's not only use to find prey or locate the food but it's also use as a defense mechanism to strike potential predators and locate their scent through the sensory of their tongue. Of course this won't be a problem if you tamed them while they are still young, this is the reason why socialization and constant handling are important so that once they grow older and larger; they will already be used to human touch and will not be aggressive.

As with most monitor lizards, if you taunt your Savannahs they could become aggressive towards you or if you are not handling them properly, they usually hiss and could strike you with their tails. In the wild, they defend themselves by running away from the predator since they are quite faster than most animals, if they got away from the enemy, they'll usually hide in trees or burrows.

Even if your Savannah monitors are socialized, docile and easy to tame you should always consider their power and never underestimate their ability to be physically dangerous. Their sharp claws and teeth could easily injure you or they can bite you if you don't know how to handle them.

They are diurnal type of creatures, which means that they are active during the day but they often dig a hole and might burrow in their substrate during hotter days.

Inside the enclosure, you can expect your pet Savannah to dig or burrow themselves underground, push around some woods or branches and sometimes find a way to escape the cage! Keep in mind that these creatures are smart and strong; the cage should be very durable otherwise they could easily break it.

Since savannah monitors grows large when it reaches adulthood, they should be housed alone and not with other types of lizards or even reptiles but if you choose to acquire more than one or two savannah monitors, you can house a male and a female or two females provided that your enclosure has a suitable amount of space that can accommodate both your pets. Never house two male savannahs otherwise they could kill each other due to territorial issues.

Keeping a Monitor Lizard

Before taking care of one, it's highly recommended that you make your loved ones comfortable with the idea of keeping a monitor lizard. You shouldn't suddenly tell your family that you'll be getting a pet monitor lizard. Learn to wait until you have familiarized them enough with monitor lizards so that they'll be comfortable to entertain the idea of living with one.

You should also be able to answer their questions about Savannah monitor lizards like the benefits of taking care of one, how much it will cost, and how big it will get. Be honest so that they will be able to assess the risks and costs of living with your potential pet. You should also show them how easy it is to maintain and take care of a Savannah monitor lizard; tell them about how other owners are having fun keeping monitor lizards as pets so your family or roommate will know that they do not have to be afraid.

You can also familiarize them with monitor lizards by showing videos, going with them to the zoo or try let them try petting one. As with all pets, you must be able to take care of your Savannah monitor lizard. You should have enough time to spend with your Savannah monitor. Assure your relatives or housemates that you are responsible enough to keep your pet lizard, and that they won't end up having to feed it for you or fight it off, if it escapes and becomes agitated. This can only be done by showing them, not just telling them, that you are a responsible keeper.

If you've tried everything you can to convince your parents or roommates but they still don't want to live with a monitor lizard, don't force them to. Even if Savannah monitor lizards aren't dangerous, people who aren't prepared to live with one may in some way agitate it. Even worse, it may cause a fight between you and your housemates.

It's not easy to convince people to live with a monitor lizard, but there is reason for them to be scared. Despite everything, monitor lizards in general are not used to people and people are almost taught to fear such creatures (for a good reason). So learn to wait until you can get your own place or until they're. Before you get your own Savannah monitor lizard, you must make sure the people you live with are okay with it, if you can't find anyone willing to support you either your roommates or family members, it is better not to take care of one at least in the meantime, otherwise you might end up having to relocate it.

Pros and Cons of Savannah Monitors

Pros

- Suited for novice keepers or beginners but prior lizard handling or experience will be best
- Mostly available in local pet shops compared to other lizard species
- They are docile and easy to tame as well as non – venomous unlike other monitor lizards.
- Safe around people provided that there is supervision and they are properly handled
- Very easy to feed, does not neglect any food and they can also digest food easily.
- Unlikely to get ill with appropriate care.
- Trouble-free shedding.
- Can live for about 15 to 20 years

- Requires no supervision, provided that its enclosure is safe and secured.

- Its food are also available in reptile shops or major pet stores

Cons

- Growth may be relatively hard to manage since it can get quite heavy and long.

- Initial cost for caging and other materials could be expensive.

- Not as receptive to humans as other animals usually kept as household pets but can be playful when handled.

- Can be easily trained, tamed, and socialize.

- May not be ideal for families with very young children

- Can live up to 20 years or more which means that long – term commitment is needed.

Monitor Lizard Licensing

The Convention on International Trade in Endangered Species (CITES) for wild fauna and flora are the governing body that is responsible in taking care of all animal species especially the endangered ones. Almost all countries in major continents all over the world are a member of CITES including USA, Europe, Latin America, Asia and Australia. It is highly recommended that you have legal or proper documents regarding any animal or species you keep as pets to save you in case of any trouble.

CITES has 3 appendices and each appendix contains a list of different species in different categories, and therefore has different rules when it comes to keeping, exporting and trading monitor lizards. Most monitor lizards including the Savannah monitors fall under the CITES II appendix. CITES II includes species that can be traded freely but cannot be taken from the wild.

You will not be allowed to transport monitor lizards from one country to another if you don't have an export certificate from CITES and from the country of origin as well as the CITES import certificate to the country of your destination. If you want to travel or transport your pet Savannah, you should have these certificates by satisfying authorities that your pet is obtained legally.

It doesn't necessarily require any approval from wildlife authorities or organizations (although it might be ideal to ask other breeders/vets about the legality of the pet). Usually, you just need to simply provide a document stating the name, identity of the species or your Savannah monitors as well as the name address, contact details and signature of the previous owner or where you bought it from. You need to also provide your own personal details and signature. This document needs to be kept for future reference.

Although commercial trade is allowed for monitor lizards listed in Appendix II including the Savannah monitors but you should still have a CITES document/approval or other form of legal permit. If you don't comply with the regulations of CITES, authorities has grounds to automatically confiscate your pet Savannah or you could pay a fine, and worse imprisonment. If you're going to buy or sell monitor lizards from other countries, you'll need an authorization for import to make sure that they will be legally imported.

Conservation Connection

Even if most monitor lizards have a 'least concern' conservation status, these reptiles are still very important to the environment and the ecosystem as a whole because they fill a role in the food chain. Monitor lizards, especially those living in the wild are also helpful in controlling agricultural pests like rodents and various types of insects. Aside from that they can also help in dispersing seeds in the wild.

What many breeders and wildlife experts are getting concerned about is the growing trend of using a monitor lizard's skin as a material for the creation of shoes, bags, boots and other fashion products. In a 10 year period, 1,000 savannah monitor skins were imported in America that was used in the production of such products. Many wildlife organizations don't recommend buying such products especially if you're in abroad to help stop these companies who are killing these reptiles.

Cost of Owning a Savannah Monitor Lizard

The overall costs for keeping a Savannah monitor lizards include those costs that you must cover before you can bring your monitor lizard home. Some of the costs you will need to cover include the enclosure or tank, food, water dishes, supplies like heaters, bulbs and misting equipment as well as cage décor or accessories, breeding materials, and even medical care (just in case). The cost will also include the cost of your Savannah lizard. It is highly recommended that you buy from online stores or websites, legit breeders as well as during any reptile conventions so you can be sure that your acquiring a healthy lizard. The tank as well as the cage materials can also be bought from fixture stores or your local hardware because if you buy from a pet store it could be more expensive.

The cost in purchasing your savannah monitors can vary greatly depending on the type of species, its age and your local area. You can probably find a backyard breeder offering $30 or below but you cannot be sure of the breeding quality for these baby monitor lizards. Quality savannah lizards sell for $20 and up. Buying from legit breeders during a reptile convention may neither be cheap or expensive.

When you purchase a savannah lizards, you need to make sure that their tank are somewhat similar to its natural habitat in the wild so that it won't have trouble adjusting to its new environment. Providing adequate shelter will make them feel at ease and comfortable as a house pet. They may need to get used to you or other people checking them out while they are inside their enclosure so make sure that the kind of cage you will buy will protect them from any dangerous threats around the house including your house pets.

Large tanks even though it may be quite time consuming in terms of cleaning it, is much suitable for your monitor lizard because it will provide ample air circulation. You can also opt to create your own cage using alternative materials like wood but you have to make sure that it's strong so that your pet won't easily break it. It could also be a great alternative if you would want to have a cheaper enclosure since wooden cage materials.

Adequate lighting, heating and misting will provide appropriate temperature and humidity levels inside your pet lizard's cage enclosure. You need to purchase things like a UVB bulb, heat bulb, other light fixtures to provide the tank with a basking area and a cooler area. You can also buy a reptile thermometer to easily help you in regulating temperatures and the cage's humidity levels.

Aside from buying food like live insects, veggies, and other gut loading foods you need to also provide supplements for your Savannah monitors, this is equivalent to vitamins for us humans to protect them against diseases and strengthen the body. You also need to install a watering system for your pet. You can use a fogger or fogging machine to also help in humidity levels or you can opt to buy an automatic misting system but it's much more expensive though it could make it easier to monitor.

Like humans, or any other pets, these reptiles do get sick and most often than not once you find out it's already worst or an emergency case already. Be sure to save up for its medical needs and vet costs. You may also need to do some medical checkups and/or lab tests once in a while for your pet. In addition to purchasing your Savannah monitor's enclosure and installing fixtures, you should also purchase cage decors such as branches, leaves, live plants and other accessories to ensure that they'll live in a familiar habitat but it's probably ideal if you don't buy a lot since Savannah monitors can easily destroy it once they grow larger although it could also help in increasing humidity.

You also need to buy a laying bin if in case you'd be breeding your Savannah monitors. You can either buy some kind of reptile container or a standard laying bin in pet stores. The breeding cost will vary depending on the quality, so you should budget about $50 or more for these extra costs.

Estimated Costs of Keeping a Savannah Monitor:

- Savannah Monitor Lizard breed: $50 - $69
- Glass Enclosure with a screen top or lid (for hatchlings): average of $99 (depending on size)
- Glass Enclosure (for adults): $250 (complete set with regulators/heaters)
- Bedding or Substrate: $6/bag
- Water Dish(for adults/large): $20 or more (depending on size/quality)

- Heaters/Misting Equipment: around $40 total or more
- Basking Lamp/UVB bulbs: $100 or more
- Heat and Water Temperature Regulator/ Gauges: $5 or more
- Hiding Spots: $5 for young Savannahs
- Temporary tank (for young Savannahs): $30 - $50 or more
- Food: $12/bag or more (depending on brand and amount/quantity)
- Laying bin: $50

Chapter Three: How to Acquire Savannah Monitor Lizards

In this chapter you will be provided with the criteria on selecting a healthy Savannah monitor breed and be given criteria to spot a reputable and trustworthy breeder. You will also learn where to legally purchase monitor lizards. It's essential that before you purchase any lizards for this matter, you should first consider on who bred and raised them. You'll also be provided with links where you can purchase a lizard online. Keep in mind that purchasing a healthy breed is one of the most essential things that every potential reptile keeper should learn about.

Where to Purchase a Savannah Monitor

This section will discuss the different places where you can purchase your own monitor lizard as well as some tips on how to avoid bad or illegal breeders.

Private breeders are a great source because these people don't just breed monitor lizards because they want to sell their pets, they do it because they just actually care for these pet species which is a great sign because it means that you're getting a monitor lizard breed that is well – taken care of and eliminates many unwanted factors when it comes to finding a reputable breeder. Of course, you also have to be careful when it comes to dealing with private breeders, make sure to do you due diligence, and ask the right questions to spot a good breeder from a bad breeder.

Another good place to buy is reptile shops are highly recommended among expert and novice monitor lizard keepers including reptile enthusiasts and veterinarians. What makes it great is that, you can go in there and ask any questions about your chosen breed. The staffs are usually very helpful and are experts when it comes to any monitor lizard species given the time they have spent with a lot of breeds.

You can also find a variety of species for a particular breed even monitor lizard species that may not be available in a standard commercial pet store, which is good because you want to have as many Savannah monitor choices as possible.

Reptile shows is another great place to buy a monitor lizard because every species that they sell is always much cheaper than pet shops and even private breeders. You can buy a healthy Savannah monitor that is cheaper than what they are usually worth which is fantastic because you'll save a lot of money, though you also need to be careful, and make sure that the people you're buying from knows what they're doing. If you choose to become a season keeper or someone who maybe just want to try keeping a monitor lizard but don't necessarily see yourself raising them for a long time, then you might want to acquire your monitor lizard from rescue centers. You can do this by checking your local rescue center.

However, the availability of a particular monitor lizard species like Savannah monitors will vary; you may not have a lot of choices when it comes to selecting a healthy breed or sometimes may not have any choice at all. Some rescue centers offer certain monitor lizard species for a minimal amount but you may need to prove to them that you'll be a good and responsible breeder. Breeders love to support rescue centers because they're the ones who are saving these species' lives, and picking up after the bad keepers.

How to Spot a Reputable Monitor Lizard Breeder

Selecting a breeder is the first step before you buy any pet because if the breeder is reputable, caring, and a responsible caregiver, you can be sure that the monitor lizard is well – taken care of. Good breeders must be knowledgeable about the breeds they raise, and should give you specific info about the breed. They have to take note that the primary reason for breeding a monitor lizard is for health or because it is their hobby, and not just for appearance or selling purposes. Breeders tend to know a lot about the species they breed so they often can supply more information than a typical pet store clerk. If they only tell you general information, chances are they're not really interested with their pets. They should be able to teach you how to properly set up the enclosure, where to place it, and the right temperature/humidity levels needed.

Legit breeders know how to establish a good relationship with their potential/existing buyers. Be sure to ask for referrals from their previous buyers so that you can ask them about the pet they've bought from this breeder, and if they have good rapport. A good breeder who is passionate about the animals that they breed will want to talk to you about them. They will not hesitate to answer your questions and at the same time ask questions of their own.

If a breeder doesn't bother to answer all of your questions in order to get you to spend money with them in the first place. Chances are that they will be unresponsive to you after the sale because reputable breeders will walk you through every step of the process. They are willing to answer all of your questions and if they think that you are not a good fit as an owner, they won't sell it to you. Yes, they want to earn money but they also want to protect the integrity of the hobby.

Some Questions You Can Ask to Spot a Good Breeder

- Can you tell me information about Savannah monitors or this particular breed?

- What are the things I need for its habitat? Any stores or brands you can refer? What kind of enclosure does it prefer?

- How did you breed the monitor lizards? How did you raise them?

- How many times should I feed it? How often? What food or brands can you recommend?

- How do I set up its habitat? What should be the temperature?

- How many years have you been in business, and what kind of experience do you have as a breeder?

- What do you specialize in? What types of species do you breed and sell?

- Do you offer any kind of a warranty or guarantee? If so, how long?

- Can I ask any referrals?

Characteristics of a Healthy Breed

Whether you choose a baby Savannah, juvenile or an adult, there are several things to keep in mind when selecting a healthy breed. The first you should look out for is the eyes; you want to look for clear eyes that are free of any discharge or cloudiness except of course, when the monitor lizard is preparing to shed. Next is the breathing; you need to look out for a healthy breathing with no signs of labor breathing and no nostril discharge. You should also opt to get a monitor lizard that has a rounded and full body and a species that is active and alert to its environment. It should not have any mobility issues, the monitor lizard should be able to move freely as well.

Never purchase or acquire a monitor lizard that has blisters on its skin or scale injuries because these are signs of ill health or inadequate environment respectively. Another sign to watch out for is parasite infestation in its scales. The monitor lizard should readily use its tongue to smell and search its environment.

When you lift it up, you should be able to feel a sense of strength to its body. It's also highly recommended that you choose a Savannah monitor that is bred in captivity, because wild Savannah monitors may carry with them health problems and parasites. They are also harder to handle since they have lived in the wild all their life, and are not used to handling or socialization.

List of Breeders and Rescue Websites

While going to a reptile pet shop or rescue center is convenient, going online to buy your Savannah monitor will save you some money. If you want to see your chosen monitor lizard up close and personal, however, you may want to opt for local breeders in your area, speak to other monitor lizard breeders or try looking for reptile or lizard forums/ online groups. The people in these groups are usually knowledgeable about reptiles and monitor lizards, and may give you good advice on where to acquire your Savannah monitor.

Here is the list of breeders and adoption rescue websites around United States and United Kingdom:

United States Breeders and Rescue Websites

Back Water Reptiles

<http://www.backwaterreptiles.com/monitor-lizards/savannah-monitor-for-sale.html

Reptile City

<http://www.reptilecity.com/Merchant2/merchant.mvc?Screen=PROD&Product_Code=BMHL&Category_Code=Monitors>

Snake at Sunset

<http://snakesatsunset.com/monitor-lizards-for-sale/>

First Choice Reptiles

<http://www.firstchoicereptiles.com/savannah-monitor-for-sale/>

Underground Reptiles

<https://undergroundreptiles.com/shop/baby-savannah-monitor/>

XYZ Reptiles

<https://www.xyzreptiles.com/baby-savannah-monitor-lizards-as-pets-learn-before-you-buy/>

Rept Mart

<http://www.reptmart.com/p-2526-savannah-monitor-for-sale.aspx>

Petco

<https://www.petco.com/content/petco/PetcoStore/en_US/pet-services/resource-center/caresheets/monitor-and-tegu.html>

Big Apple Herp

<http://www.bigappleherp.com/Savannah-Monitor>

Beautiful Dragons Reptile Rescue

<http://www.beautifuldragons.com/rescue.html>

Arrowhead Reptile Rescue

<http://www.arrowheadreptilerescue.org/>

Preloved UK

<http://www.preloved.co.uk/classifieds/pets/reptiles/all/uk/bosc+monitor>

Gumtree

<https://www.gumtree.com/reptiles/uk/bosc+monitor>

Urban – Exotics UK

<http://www.urban-exotics.co.uk/monitor-lizards-for-sale.html>

Pets for Homes UK

<https://www.pets4homes.co.uk/sale/reptiles/monitor/>

Sunny Side Lizard Rescue UK

<http://sunnysidelizardrescue.weebly.com/>

Chapter Four: Setting Up a Habitat for Your Savannah Monitor Lizard

So now you have decided to purchase a Savannah monitor lizard because you have probably seen some cool videos and/or some of your friends might have them, the first thing you need to consider and think about is its caging and habitat requirements. Before you learn how to feed them, handle them or even breed them, you should first and foremost have knowledge about its environmental needs like how to house them, the materials you should use, and other housing tips you'll need to know to ensure that they will be happily living in their new home and so that they can easily adapt to a new environment in order to avoid being stressed out.

Cage Considerations for Savannah Monitor Lizards

When it comes to buying a cage, the first thing you need to know is the size of the hutch or housing you're going to need. Of course, this will depend on how large or small your savannah monitor lizard is when you acquire them, but you also need to keep in mind their growth rate and other basking factors that they'll need which your cage should provide. You need to keep in mind the length and the height of the enclosure as well as the heat equipment that will be attached to the cage.

Ideally, the temporary cage for a baby Savannah monitor lizard should be a 55 – gallon tank, and once it becomes an adult the cage size should at least be 6 feet in length, 3 to 4 feet in height and 4 to 6 feet in depth. As with most animals, the general rule of thumb is the bigger, the better.

Since Savannah monitor lizards can grow big and long over time, it's probably more practical and economical for you if you buy a cage that's about twice or thrice its size or the ideal measures given, so that once it grows up, you don't need to get another enclosure to accommodate its size. Savannah monitor lizards are also an animal that likes to roam around, is curious about its surroundings, and a species that is naturally used to exploring the wildlife which is why it's best to purchase a relatively large size enclosure so that they can have plenty of space to walk around just like how they do it in the wild.

You should also keep in mind that even though Savannah monitor lizards are the most docile monitor species, they are still fond of escaping! They will find their way out of the cage or even create a new way out which is why you need to make sure that the enclosure you will buy or build is either made out of thick glass/plexiglass or thick plywood because these animals have very sharp claws that can easily rip the enclosure apart if it's made out of mesh or low quality materials. The last thing you'll want to know is that your Savannah monitor is on the loose!

Another important factor when you're picking out an enclosure is the ease of access, you don't want to buy very large materials to put inside a cage if the enclosure itself doesn't have a wide opening or somewhat hard to access. You can also opt to purchase a glass tank since it's much affordable and provides an accessible sliding doors or glass lids.

If you purchase a temporary glass enclosure that comes with a screen top lid for baby species, it doesn't necessarily mean that your monitor lizard will die but you have to make sure that you closely monitor the temperatures and humidity of the cage. Ideally, your Savannah monitor should have a basking temperature of about 130 degrees or so, that way they can digest larger preys.

Substrate

When it comes to maintaining humidity inside a glass type of enclosure, you'll need a thick layer of substrate. You can either use a coconut type of bedding or a bark substrate; you can also choose to combine them because it can help provide a lot of moisture and humidity. You can also make a thick layer so that your pet monitor lizard can burrow into it.

Spag Moss/Plants

If you have a large size enclosure, you should also purchase lots of spag moss. Two to three pack of spag moss is perfect to spread it out on your large cage. Spag moss is use to absorb a lot of moisture, and it also doesn't become a breeding ground for molds which means that it is quite durable and can be used for a long time. You can also mix it up with your bedding or substrate so your monitor lizard can get another type of texture or layer as well as an addition in maintaining humidity. When it comes to plants, it may temporarily be good for your enclosure. A baby Savannah lizard is already huge enough to easily crush the plants you'll provide, so if you wanted to put some plants for aesthetic or humidity purposes don't buy lots of it or some kind of an expensive plant because it will be destroyed as your pet grows larger.

Water bowls

It's important for monitor species like the Savannah monitor lizard to have a relatively huge water bowl because this is where they are going to soak their bodies into as well as defecate. Since Savannah monitor lizards are relatively large kind of species, you should provide an extra-large sized water bowl for it especially once it reaches its full size. For baby lizards, you can choose to fill the bowl halfway if you're worried about it being too deep and your pet could be drowning. You could change the water bowl either every day or at least every other day so that it won't be too dirty or contaminated for your monitor lizard otherwise it could make them ill since bacteria could harbor and begin to dwell in the water bowl.

Fogger/ Misting equipment for Enclosures

In addition to a humid cage, you can use foggers or a misting equipment on top of your pet's enclosure to maintain high humidity anytime of the day since it has a built – in timer.

Types of Hiding Spots and Where to Place Them inside the Cage

When choosing a hiding spot, you should consider the age and current size of your monitor lizard. If you acquire a baby Savannah monitor lizard, they could adapt more easily if the enclosure has more foliage and hiding areas. Another important factor is the location of the hiding cave or hiding area inside the enclosure because if for example, you purchase a sort of closed type of hiding spot and you put it directly under the heating equipment, it could heat your pet too much and they can be in an uncomfortable state and of course, you won't be able to regulate the temperature inside. Try to purchase a hiding spot that has some opening on it so you can also provide some branches where they can bask on. You should also place it in the pool side or near the water bowl or on the cooler side of the enclosure.

When it comes to choosing a hiding spot, the aesthetic and quality of the hiding area is also important because it won't only look cool from the outside but will also make your pet monitor lizard comfortable on the inside. Design wise, you can choose from various style found in different local pet shops like a skull design, dinosaur egg style, rock type of hiding spots and other sturdy rock - looking materials. In this section, we'll show you different kinds of hiding spots you can purchase for your Savannah monitor lizard:

Stacked Up Type of Hiding Spot – this kind of hiding spot is sort of like rocks that had been stacked up, has levels of hiding areas and also has many openings. This is a great design because you can put it under a heater or light without your pet getting heat up too much. The top spot is the warmest area and as it goes lower through other levels, the temperature drops which can provide your lizard with an option to regulate temperature.

Hut Type of Hiding Spot – brands like the Habba hut are one of the typical hiding spots not just for monitor lizards but also for reptile pets in general such as snake, chameleons and the like. It's just a regular and simple looking inside hive that has an opening on both ends. It is also great for terrestrial type of species like the Savannah monitors or even for arboreal lizards. You can place it vertically and lean it on the side of the enclosure or the glass or you can opt to sort of dig it into the substrate.

Cork Rounds – this is mostly used for arboreal type of monitor lizards since it's hollow on the inside which provides a great hiding spot, and lizards can also bask on its openings.

Close cave type of hiding spots – its big opening in the front is suitable to fit your Savannah monitors once it gets bigger or when it reaches its maximum size. It's a great option if you're looking for a big and naturalistic type of hiding spot compared to buying plastic tubs hiding. This type of hiding material is mostly used for growing monitors; these are usually big and it provides an area where your pet can feel safe and secure.

Lighting and Heating Equipment

One of the most important things that your Savannah monitor lizard needs is heat. You can choose from different kinds of basking light; there are some products out there that provides bright lights which could help your lizard, some other types include a ceramic heater which could provide a lot more heat and could easily heat up a larger space or big enclosures, another one is called a halogen bulbs which is good for UVA because it helps your lizard to have a better color. You can also purchase a rheostat which can control up to a 250 watts lighting, it can also aid in regulating temperature if you bought a light that is not UVB.

Types of Lighting/Heating Equipment

Ceramic Heaters – this kind of heating equipment will obviously not give off any light, it only provides nothing but pure heat. It's very heavy duty, and this kind of heater is also long – lasting (unless the brand you purchase is not a quality type of heater.)

Halogen Bulbs – aside from providing a UVA for your lizard that could aid in its skin color, you can also use halogen bulbs. This kind of equipment is very hot and very bright which is why a lot of monitor lizard keepers use it. If you purchase 50 watt bulbs, you can just have two or three of it, and put it over a section of the cage providing your pet with a basking zone. This is also suitable for larger type of monitors like the Savannah monitor because it's a lot safer. Buying two or three of these halogen bulbs is better than just purchasing one thick bulb; this is because a thick bulb can create a hot spot or even burn your pet whereas the three bulb spread across a portion of the enclosure is much more ideal in providing the needed temperature in the basking area. The downside is that halogen bulbs tends to break easily if it is moved too much, so you need to be really careful and make sure that if you're going to place/attach them in the enclosure it won't be moved a lot because it can break faster.

Basking Bulbs – this type of bulbs are the cheapest, it only costs around $15 or less, quite durable (depending on the brand quality) and also perfect in heating as well as providing light for your pet monitor lizard.

UVB Light – it has a big hot light bulb that provides lots of heat and has lots of UV lighting. UVB lighting is highly recommended since most monitor lizards including Savannah species are helophytic and they thrive with more ultra violet lighting. Although there are lots of keepers that don't use UVB, it's best especially for newbies and first time Savannah lizard owners to purchase a UVB type of lighting or some sort of mercury vapor bulb to make it easier for you. It also helps in the absorption of vitamins and nutrition from their gut – loaded foods. UVB lighting mimic natural conditions like the sun's heat which is perfect for monitor lizards in captivity.

Heat Pads – You can also purchase heat pads and attached it to the bottom of the enclosure to warm your pet. All you have to do is to stick it on the very far end of the enclosure or as far away to the water dish as possible. Since heat pads have rubber feet, you have to ensure that they are safely attached in all the four corners to allow air circulation otherwise; the heat could be trapped under the tank and could be too hot for your pet monitor. You can leave it on for the whole day. If you choose to use this, you may not need to buy many bulbs, just make sure to regulate the heat and light temperature.

Chapter Five: Diet for Your Savannah Monitor Lizard

Savannah monitors are insectivores and carnivores. However, there had been some debate among zoologists and keepers whether or not these creatures should be fed with a mix of insects and thawed meat or an insect type of diet only. While some keepers do feed their pet monitors a strict insect diet, it's highly recommended that you feed your pet monitor with a variety of food because in the wild they eat different kinds of insects, lizards, birds, rodents as well as eggs of other reptile species or their own kind.

In this chapter, you'll learn the different types of food for your Savannah monitor lizard, some feeding tips as well as feeding amount and frequency so that they can have a balanced – diet meal.

Nutrition in the Wild vs. In Captivity

Savannah monitor lizards are scavengers and natural hunters in the wild; they usually eat a lot during the wet season but during the dry season they also live off some fat reserves. Since Savannah monitors are captive pets, they will now spend most of their lives inside a cage or enclosure and food will be available to them without doing any type of hunting (unless of course you have a desert – like backyard for these creatures), this is where the problem starts for these creatures because it can often times result into obesity and the development of other health illnesses like digestive diseases especially if you will give them more than the amount of food required for their age or size.

Some Savannah monitor keepers give cat foods and even dog foods; cat or dog foods as well as other type of species diet should be avoided because it may contain ingredients that are toxic to reptiles or monitor lizards in general. However, some vets and keepers have proven dog foods to be effective for underweight baby Savannah monitors as well as those that are ill although you might need to consult your vet first before giving any because dog foods also contain high levels of fats that could be too much for your monitor's diet.

Savannah monitors that are zoo – captives are often being fed with raw and low fat turkey, eggs as well as some supplements that are mixed suitably for optimum health, so you can also choose to feed your pet with these types of diet although you should be very careful because salmonella bacteria can become a problem and are dangerous to both of you.

You can buy ready to eat or commercial savannah lizard diet in your local pet stores but of course it should never be the entire diet of your pet. Fresh thawed foods and live insects should also be given to constitute a healthy diet.

How Monitor Lizards Eat in the Wild

In the wild, monitor lizards like the docile Savannah monitor is a top predator. They will hunt anything that is smaller (and sometimes quite bigger) than them, sometimes they'll also prey on their own kin.

When hunting for food, they just don't follow their prey's scent, they think ahead! Most monitor lizards are smart, they calculate everything they do including how to find their prey or escape from a predator. They naturally learn and memorize all major landmarks around; they read their surroundings and look at it like a map. In the wild, they are known to surprise their prey by taking shortcuts to its hideout and ambush other animals in order to save their energy, so instead of chasing these animals, they find their victim's location and prowl on it without even breaking a sweat.

Most monitor lizards in the wild follows trails of other species or potential prey relentlessly using their special senses that guides them and enables them to locate their prey with accuracy. What's special about their olfactory sense is that they can identify the scent of a particular animal they wanted to follow or eat even if it's combine with other scents of animals who passed by in the same area. As mentioned earlier, they use their forked tongue in making sense of their environment like snakes, and perhaps the best use for it is to follow the scent of their food. Every time they pull in their tongues, they read this scents with the organ located in their upper mouth, it's like tasting and smelling at the same time. The forked tongue also enables them to know how long ago the prey has passed in a particular area and identify which way it's heading! As long as there is a traceable scent, monitor lizards follow it even under the ground.

Diet for Your Savannah Monitor Lizard

The majority of your pet's nutrition should be insects as well as thawed or frozen mice; you can also choose to supplement their food with pre – killed mice. Don't feed your lizard with a live rodent because it can harm or cause injury to your Savannah monitor and also prompt him/her to be afraid or to stop feeding. Thawed mice/rodents and small insects like crickets, roaches, mealworms, wax worms and kingworms that are gut – loaded are the safest food to feed your Savannah monitor lizard. Adult monitor lizard can easily consume an adult mouse, and they rarely eat a prey that quite huge for them, if they do they might regurgitate it. Feeding them insects can be ideal because chasing these live insect preys also provides an opportunity for exercise even if they're inside an enclosure. For baby Savannahs you can feed them with a small mouse that's about the size of a pinkie and then gradually feed them with fuzzy rodents as they grow.

Insects that are caught in the wild including lightning bugs are not advisable as part of your monitor's diet because these insects could carry diseases. When it comes to the size of the prey, you should make sure that it is not too big for your pet – the guideline for this is that it shouldn't be longer than the distance of your monitor's eyes or the longer than the distance between its nose and eyes. Otherwise, you could chop them up for your pet or even molt them to avoid digestion problems and impactions due to exoskeleton of some insects or their hard shells.

Feeding Amount and Frequency

Adult Savannah Monitors: for pets that are longer than 3 feet, they should be fed at least 2 to 3 times in a week, while juveniles should be fed more often since they need more food to aid in their growth. All uneaten food should be immediately remove from the cage especially if they are live insects because they can bite your pet and also cause some injuries. This is why savannah monitor keepers also recommend feeding their pets in a separate cage because they can easily see if their lizard leaves any food behind without having to inspect all the materials inside the enclosure.

- Baby Savannahs that are about 1 foot long should be fed with 4 fuzzy mice every 2 to 3 days.
- Juveniles around 3 feet long should be fed 1 to 4 thawed mice at least twice a week
- Adults that are more than 3 feet should be fed 2 to 3 mice, once or twice a week.

How to Dust Your Lizard's Food

Most vets recommended that you properly feed the insects or the prey a special diet or good nutrition so that in the end your pet monitor lizard will benefit from that very balanced and proper nutrition. In order for you to gut load the food of your Savannah lizard you should supplement it with a multivitamin powder with calcium.

Unfortunately, most commercial gut loads are low in calcium which may not be sufficient for your monitor lizard's nutritional needs. The great thing is that you can actually gut load your pet's diet yourself to make sure that it contains the needed nutrients. It's very easy to make and quite inexpensive.

Calcium is very important to your Savannah monitor's diet as well as the vitamins that can be found in powdered supplements. You should sprinkle or dust a small amount of these powdered supplements in the feeder insect before giving them to your pet lizard. Use calcium twice a week, as well as calcium with D3 and a multivitamin at least once a month. The time wherein you should feed your insects to your monitor lizard should be no more than twelve hours from the time you gut load it. Keep in mind that inadequate dietary calcium leads to metabolic bone disease, a very serious and potentially fatal reptile illness.

Chapter Six: Husbandry for Savannah Monitor Lizards

Savannah monitors are cold – blooded and ectothermic species which means that their own body temperature depends and adapts to the temperature of their environment. Part of good husbandry for this docile yet exotic species is to ensure that their environment have just the right kind of warm and cool temperature so that they can properly shed, absorb their food, and live healthily. Maintenance of a clean and good environment inside their enclosure is a must! In this chapter you'll learn the right temperatures for your pet Savannah as well as some housing maintenance tips.

Cage Temperatures and Humidity

Your monitor's cage temperature should always be regulated and/or monitored to ensure that they have the right humidity levels. You can purchase a reptile or cage thermometer in checking the temperatures of the enclosure's different areas. As mentioned from previous chapters, you can purchase different types of light bulbs or heaters to see what works best for you and your Savannah monitor.

The warm side of the enclosure should ideally be at 85 to 90 degrees Fahrenheit; the cool side should at least be at 80 degrees while the basking area (where the heat pads/bulbs are located) should be at 100 to 120 degrees Fahrenheit. The cage humidity's basking area should be low, while the cooler area where the hiding spot is usually located should have a high percentage of humidity level.

If the room temperature is 75 degrees and below at night, you may want to use a supplemental ceramic heater; these heaters do not provide light like halogen or UVB bulbs so you don't really have to worry turning it on at night, your monitor lizard won't be disturb because these equipment only emits the needed supplemental heat. A word of caution though, if your pet Savannah will not be provided with the right lighting and heating temperature together with the UVB light, it could contribute to various health issues like respiratory diseases or symptoms, metabolic bone disorders (very common illnesses among reptiles in general) and may completely stop eating because improper environmental temperatures could cause them to have a difficulty in digesting their food.

Light and Heating Cycles

To maintain your Savannah monitor's biological rhythm or natural day and night patterns just like in the wild, you should make sure that they have at least 8 to 12 daytime and nighttime hours. You have to make sure that you adjust the settings of your light and heating cycles so that your pet can identify night and day since they will be mostly be in their enclosures inside your house. The daylight hours and seasons change, sometimes we have long days or long nights, that should also reflect on your pet's enclosure. Always keep in mind that the "mornings" must be light, while the "evenings" should really be dark to maintain their biological rhythm.

Habitat Maintenance Tips

- Spot cleaning is very important because it means that you thoroughly clean not just the cage of your lizard but also all the materials you placed inside the cage.

You need to clean your Savannah monitor's habitat enclosure regularly as well.

- As mentioned earlier, the humidity within the enclosure can be a perfect breeding ground for the growth of bacteria. Most reptiles can be prone to skin and bacterial infection if left alone in unclean surroundings for long which is why regular cage maintenance and cleaning should be part of your routine.

- Regular cleaning prevents the possible transmission of diseases which can be found in the fecal matter of reptiles, and which may be transmissible to humans. Not only will this keep the interior of the enclosure clean, odor-free, and healthy, but it will also keep you and your family safe and healthy.

- Spot cleaning the interior of the cage should be done as often as possible – at least once a day or once every other day. When you spot clean your pet's enclosure, you should make sure that any fecal matter is removed, the shedded skin is removed as well as the uneaten or left over food. The water bowls should also be replaced more than once a week to prevent bacterial growth.

- During the cleaning process, you will need to relocate the lizard so that you can clean and sterilize the entire tank components such as its hiding spots, substrate, plants/branches etc.

- You may need to temporarily relocate your Savannah monitor to a different tank. As usual, make sure that this cage is secure and clean, and is sufficiently ventilated.

- Before doing a full cleanse of your pet's tank, you must first find a suitable temporary cage for your monitor lizard. Check the components you need to clean and replace such as the bedding of the cage.

Chapter Seven: Handling Your Pet Monitor Lizard

Handling this kind of species that weighs about 150 pounds and has an average length of 4 feet long is something that newbies usually have a difficulty doing. Even if they are still juvenile, their sharp claws and powerful bodies could cause you injury, and could also cause them to be stressed if they are not being handled properly. Improper and sometimes inappropriate handling will make these creatures feel unsafe and uncomfortable, and it could cause potential aggression as well. In this chapter, you'll learn some techniques on how you to handle your pet Savannah and also some things about its shedding process.

Handling and the Hygiene of Your Pet

Just like other mammals or household pets such as cats, dogs and even snakes, monitor lizards should be socialized at a young age. Most savannah monitors are great for beginners because they are one of the most docile monitor lizards out there. Handling them actually depends on how domesticated these animals are, so if you acquire a baby Savannah monitor or it was born captive they'll be easier to handle and tame since you as the keeper can introduce them the concept of socialization. Regularly touching them while they are still young will make them get used to you and your scent.

The technique is to reinforce to these creatures that you're not going to harm them in anyway. So what you can do is slowly put your arms down so they can climb over it or grab them on their bellies underneath slowly and support their bodies using both hands and arms. It's better to handle them on the side of their bodies and not in front of the head or on top because that's how predators move, and they could mistake you as the enemy. Don't forget to support their hind legs and forelegs because they would feel safe and comfortable that way.

Once you do, you can then start scratching or petting its back, the top of their head, their ears and even their chins.

One way of knowing if you're doing it right is if of course, they're not trying to get away from you or becoming aggressive towards you, you can also know if they're being handled properly by their deep breathings because usually if they starts to hiss or inflate their throats that means they are uncomfortable or you're not handling them properly.

You can also make them come to you by offering some food using a spoon, once they get to identify the scent they could probably grab a bite out of it, and once they do, you can slowly slide your fingers behind the food so that he'll also be familiarized with your scent and a food scent. You sort of need to let him be attracted with the food but don't ever try to put the food in your fingers or hand feed them because they won't be able to distinguish the food and your hand!

If you continue to reinforce them especially at a young age that it's okay to jump up on you not only will it be imprinted on their minds about this socialization technique, they could pass this habituated trait from one generation to another.

Savannah monitors and all monitor lizards in general have really sharp claws, so if you're a beginner or have never had an experience in handling these types of animals before, don't be shock if they climb all over you using their claws and end up bleeding a bit because of punctured skin because in the wild, they use these claws to climb into the tree branches so it's basically natural instinct, this is just how they get around and that's something you better get used to.

Here are some reminders when handling your pet Savannah monitor lizard:

- Whatever action you take in handling or hand – feeding your monitor lizard is going to be imprinted in its mind forever (remember these creatures are intelligent).

- It's important that baby Savannah monitors get used to being having regular human contact or socializing them at a young age so that they can be tamed when they grow older.

- Some keepers put an item of clothing because it helps your pet to know your scent and gets to be comfortable whenever you're trying to handle them.

- Avoid "death grabs," as mentioned earlier; these animals in the wild have natural instincts when it comes to becoming a prey or a predator. If you handle or try to grab them directly from the top at a vertical angle, they may mistake you as a predator and this could result to potential aggression or your pet will be scared if it's still a baby. Death grabs pretty much mimic a bird in the wild or some kind of predator ready to snatch them or tackle them.

- Hissing and puffing is normal at first because your pet is still trying to get to know you and your scent, so like any other pets you have to convince them that you are a friend but expect them to be very wary at you.

- You can use a food treat to get them to come to you and once they do, you can slowly reward them by petting or rubbing them to reinforce that kind of behavior and let them know that they are not going to be eaten or harmed.

Grooming Your Pet

Monitor lizards and reptiles in general don't need any grooming compared to usual household pets. When it comes to grooming, they pretty much will take care of it by themselves, naturally. Just like most reptiles, Savannah monitors sheds which means that they can grow a new skin while their old skin eventually falls off on its own (more on shedding later). Your monitor won't also need nail trimming because with the right furnishings it will prevent the nails from overgrowing. Some keepers give their lizards a scrub on its back, you can try doing that with your Savannah but make sure you use cleaning materials that are safe and non – toxic.

When it comes to its hygiene, the thing you should watch out for is parasites. Every once in a while, it's recommended to check your pet for parasites to avoid any kinds of illnesses later on; you should also make sure that the enclosure is clean to avoid being harbored with bacteria, and that the water in its dish are regularly replace. Proper husbandry will prevent any parasite infestations and also keep a healthy hygiene for your monitor lizard.

Monitor Lizard Shedding

As mentioned earlier, monitor lizards shed their skin but compared to snakes, they don't do it as a whole piece but as patches. When your Savannah lizard begins shedding, they may usually look dull and their eyelids could at a period of time look like the eyes of a bull – frog this is all natural. Don't ever try to peel off the skin because it will naturally shed on its own, peeling could be really painful for your pet. Usually, monitor lizards shed around four to six weeks, and more often if the environment has the right temperature and humidity levels. Once it does, the shedded skin will usually be eaten by the lizard itself.

In the wild, most monitor lizards have an easier time shedding because the environment is right, and they have access to bodies of water. Shedding is needed because it enables them to grow a new layer of covering, just like with humans, our dry skin cells are constantly replace whenever we take a bath and scrub our bodies, of course, reptiles cannot be groomed so this is their natural way of doing it.

Once the new skin forms, it will begin to separate from the old layer, and it will eventually fall off into patches. There will be a fluid like layer between the new and old skin which will aid in the shedding process. So if your monitor's cage is too dry, the fluid will not properly form and will be difficult for your pet to shed.

If you want to create a more humid enclosure, you can mist it twice a day whenever it's time for your pet to shed or you can use fogging equipment or misting fixtures to make it automatic. Some keepers also provide a moist box for their pet during the shedding period. This could be a container that is cover with moist spag moss that is not watery. You can then place it near the heating pad of your enclosure; and it should also be big enough to fit your monitor lizard so that he/she can go anytime he/she wants.

Chapter Eight: Breeding Your Savannah Monitor Lizard

In this chapter you'll be provided with information about how to identify the sex of your Savannah monitor lizards as well as some breeding basics like how to set up breeding conditions, incubation, hatching and egg removal process. Before you can breed a monitor lizard, you have to familiarize yourself with your pet, learn more about its biology, its breeding behavior and also ask help from other breeders, veterinarian or attend reptile conferences so that you can have knowledge on how to successfully breed them and become a reputable breeder yourself.

Sexual Dimorphism

Savannah monitor species are dimorphic animals which means their sex can be identified easily through physical characteristics and for monitor lizards in general, sometimes males can be distinguish from females through behavioral traits. Savannah monitor lizard males have usually longer heads and a bit angular face than females; they also possess a relatively larger or longer body structure than the female and a more substantial tail base. Most female savannah monitors have a roundish body structure, their tail base is usually narrower and it is tapering inward.

How to Set Up the Right Breeding Conditions

The right environmental and feeding conditions will help your savannah monitors to procreate. You can either feed your pets in the morning and have a basking spot that is on for 24/7 or just keep the light on whenever you feed them, of course it's up to you but that will generally help your monitors when it's time to breed. If you can keep a female and a male's metabolism going every day, biologically they will feel comfortable enough to breed and support life for their offspring. Most monitor lizards have huge amount of control over biological functions including their reproduction. Some savannah monitors produce more than the average eggs, other may have less. Savannah monitor lizards usually lays about 15 to 20 eggs on average, so if your pet only laid eggs that is less than the average, you might need to improve your living condition for them or how you feed them. If they are not in an enclosure that's big enough and doesn't have enough soaking area or you don't feed them appropriately it will make their biological function activate and they'll think that since this is the conditions of their surroundings, they can only sustain life comfortably for a few offspring.

A sign that your female is ready to mate is when it gets a bit heavier because that means that the egg are developing. You can begin feeding them 3 to 4 times a week, you have to feed your females more frequently plus make sure that you provide them with higher dosage of vitamin D3 because they will also need that in the reproduction process.

How to Breed Savannah Monitor Lizards

Introduce a male to your female savannah in about 2 to 3 weeks to get your female monitor to start cycling. After doing that you can wait another week and just let them be in their cage. If in case, no mating has happened, you can introduce another male and just keep doing that kind of process until a mating happens but you need to let a male stay for at least a week or more just so they can get to know each other, and if nothing happens you can just replace it with another male and wait for another week or so. Don't rush when it comes to replacing a male species because it could stress out a female.

The reason why you need to introduce male savannah species before your female's cycle begins is because since they have complete control over their biological functions which includes their reproduction system, your female monitor can lay their eggs even before it enters her oviduct and just flush it out of the system because they don't see a male around. To them, this means that their eggs won't be fertilized because there's no one there and so they just released it before their breeding cycle starts. So to prevent that, you can introduce a male inside the enclosure but you don't let them breed, it's just more of telling your female that there's a male around so that she'll create more follicles and be receptive when you bring another male monitor that way she can go to her full breeding cycle.

You also have to make sure that the timing is right. You should be able to mark in your calendars the time you put a male in the enclosure so you can monitor the time period and when she laid her eggs.

Once they mate, you can just leave them in their enclosures for a few weeks (around 14 days or so) and just let them continue breeding. It might take about a month after mating before females lay their eggs. Proper mating happens when a male monitor mounts the female monitor on its back, when their tails with cloaca contort that means they can begin copulating. Usually it takes about a minute to an hour. After mating, the males should ideally be separated.

If you're going to have a female savannah monitor and a male in the same enclosure, make sure that you have a lay box or lay bin that you can remove from the cage because it will also remove the protectiveness in that space where she laid her eggs.

Egg Removal, Incubation and Hatching of Eggs

Around 21 to 30 days after mating, the female lizard will start burrowing because this is where she will lay her eggs, just like how they do it in the wild. So make sure that if you're going to breed them you have 3 feet of bedding or soil substrate because that's where she'll excavate.

On average savannah monitor lizards lay a clutch containing 20 eggs, but some savannah monitors can lay up to 40 eggs or more. Once your pet is done in burrowing her eggs and filling the nest, you can then carefully remove it and then place it in an incubator or under a basking lamp. If you just leave these eggs, the mother itself or your other savannah monitor lizards will dig and eat them up!

Just be careful if you're going to transfer the egg from the enclosure to an incubator, never rotate them because it could cause the embryo to suffocate inside. You can incubate them through a mixture of soil, sand, vermiculite and other potting/ground materials. The soil should be a bit damp just like clay; the important thing is that the soil that you're going to use should hold enough water but not too much because the eggs could drown in it.

If you're going to place them inside a laying bin (which is highly recommended) it should have enough space in between the eggs and to the side of the container (at least half an inch will do). You should put the laying bin in a war, or dark area like a closet and the temperature should be maintained at 80 to 88 degrees Fahrenheit.

The eggs should be whitish in color, if the eggs are yellow or brown in color that means that the babies are dead, remove this dead eggs immediately. Never try to cut open the eggs or turn them because they will hatch on their own time individually. The incubation period is about 5 to 6 months; the eggs also hatch within just a few hours apart.

Raising Savannah Monitor Lizards

You should set up your new savannah hatchlings in groups of two or three and put them in a tank that is at least 18 inches in length, 12 inches wide and 3 feet in height. You can also purchase a tank that's about 15 gallon or follow what we've discuss in the habitat requirements chapter. You should also provide them with hiding spots and branches so they can have an exercise through climbing. Don't forget to place a water dish with clean water to soak in as well as proper temperature levels. Feed them gut – loaded foods like live insects that are smaller than them and follow the frequency guidelines as we've discussed in the feeding or nutrition chapter.

When your baby Savannahs reached 5 inches that means they're becoming juveniles and will continue to grow larger over time, you can start moving them to a larger enclosure of their own or keep at least 2 females per enclosure.

Life Cycle of a Monitor Lizard

The female savannah will lay the eggs once it has been fertilized. They usually dig holes for them to lay upon and they keep their eggs under the substrate. The mother will now begin looking after its eggs until those eggs hatch; the shell of their eggs has quite a hard texture. For those who are breeding savannah monitors, you can help their eggs hatch by putting it under proper lighting or heating temperature, you can consult other breeders or your vet for the proper temperature for that your monitor species.

The young hatchling will obtain its food from the egg yolk until it comes out of the shell. Once the incubation period is done, the young savannah monitors will begin to bite the egg of its shell, and start eating thawed food or small mealworms from then on and also begin shedding. Juvenile savannah monitors will reach sexual maturity around 1 ½ years old.

Chapter Nine: Common Diseases and Treatments

Monitor lizards in general might look like an animal that could never get sick, I mean they're predators right? They're born in the wild; their mothers left them at an early age, they survive on their own even when they were just hatchlings, they know how to hunt for their own food, and most of the time if they encounter another predator they usually isn't scared of it because that's how confident they are with themselves. But just like any other 'beastly' looking creatures in the wild and even in captivity, these animals don't appear weak or at least they don't let you know it because that's their natural instinct and also a part of their defense mechanism to protect themselves against potential predators. Little did we know, they're already hurting inside but they don't show it because they have a need to survive.

In this chapter, we will take a look at some illness that is very common among monitor lizards in general so that you can prevent them from getting sick and also keep them healthy.

Minor Illness

Intestinal Parasites

Intestinal parasites are composed of microscopic worms and protozoa that basically live inside your lizard's intestine. These kinds of parasites are very common among captive bred Savannah monitor. Intestinal parasites are usually acquired from ingesting an infected or contaminated feeder as well as infected feces from other animals. The usual signs of intestinal parasites are smelly feces, lethargy, weight loss and lack of appetite as well as vomiting. These parasites are microscopic and therefore can't be seen by the naked eye, that's why you need to bring in a fresh fecal sample for laboratory analysis. Usually deworming medications are prescribed but it's not a one – size – fit – all, it still depends on the kind of parasite living inside your monitor lizard. A fecal sample is taken to find eggs of the parasites, however sometimes worms are don't shed eggs so a negative fecal test doesn't necessarily mean that your pet is free from parasites. Several fecal tests or samples should be submitted.

Parasite infestation is very common among monitor lizards. This don't just affect one species, it could also affect other lizard species if ever you have more than one, and it can also be associated with other illnesses. The parasites should be identified immediately so that proper treatment can be given. Parasites sucks blood from its host and can be potentially life – threatening if there's already a swarm of mites or ticks in your Savannah which could eventually cause loss of blood. Aside from that, these parasites can also transfer a disease from one animal species to another enabling other bacterial or viral diseases enter your pet's bloodstream.

Parasite infestation is mainly because of unsanitary living conditions, imports, and improper husbandry. Parasites can usually be found on pets imported from other countries that are not properly quarantined or may not be quarantined at all. This will cause it to spread in the whole collection and transfer from one species to another. If you are acquiring a savannah monitor lizard from other countries, you have to make sure that it is properly quarantined; otherwise you will risk the lives of your other snakes or other reptile collections if any. Parasites also serve as vectors for other disease causing agents like bacteria that causes pneumonia and infectious stomatitis. They could just be found under the scales of your savannah monitors and other parts of its body.

If you notice your pet having a bland appearance it might already be infested with mites. You should check areas around its eyes, its cloaca or its back because this is where most parasites accumulate. If you have a large pet collection parasites could be difficult to remove if not prevented. Make sure that even after your monitor lizard is free of these mites or ticks their enclosure is free of it completely. You have to spot clean and thoroughly treat the entire enclosure or tank. If the environment is not properly cleaned or treated, parasites can potentially accumulate and infest your pet again. They are a source of further disease but if you diagnosed it as soon as possible, it can be given proper treatment and eventually be exterminated from your pet.

Major Illnesses

Fatty Liver Disease

Fatty liver disease is one of the most common conditions among monitor lizards. If your savannah monitor's liver accumulated too much fats it would not be able to function properly and could also cause other digestive problems. The main culprit of this disease is inappropriate feeding diet as well as lack of exercise (since they're pretty much just inside an enclosure) and too much food. The usual signs of a fatty liver include a yellowish skin, gums and eyes as well as sluggish and lethargic appearance or behavior.

The main function of the liver in monitor lizards is to break down toxins, so if this organ will not properly function due to excess fats, the toxic waste could build up and cause the bile of your lizard to breakdown. The bile has a yellowish substance called bilirubin and when it enters the blood stream it could cause jaundice. This is also the reason why monitor lizards suffering from this disease exhibits a yellowish gums or skin color. When an obese monitor lizard suddenly doesn't eat anymore, the fats will be stored to keep the metabolic activity going but if there's an influx or too much fat in the liver it will still store it but that's where the problem will start simply because there's no room left.

If you're pet has a liver problem, it will stress him/her out and also cause the immune system to become weak leaving your pet predispose to other conditions and also bacterial or fungal infestations. Obesity can also cause the lizard to have a fatty liver disease which is why you should lessen feeding it with animals that is heavy in fats.

Most of the time, owners notice signs of a fatty liver when it's already too late, fatty liver could also cause diabetes and cushing's disease. The vet will usually test the history of your pet, its diet as well as its feeding frequency, amount and the size of its enclosure so be sure to be aware of that.

The treatment for fatty liver is force – feeding your pet to eat, this seems quite ironic but the science behind it is that the fat is going to the liver because the animal is not eating which will force the body to store fats in the liver to keep the species active or metabolize. If you force feed the lizard, it will make the body stop storing fats to its liver and will at least alleviate the problem.

Vets will usually recommend a medication such as corticosteroids, some vitamins and perhaps a guideline of the proper diet or feeding amount for your monitor lizard so that it can recover. However, if the liver is already at its worst condition which means that if the toxins have already built up in the lizard's bloodstream and is causing other illnesses, it won't most likely recover and may need to be euthanized.

As a keeper, if you want to prevent a fatty liver disease, you should make sure that your pet monitor is eating the right kind of diet and the appropriate amount for its size or age. You should also be able to provide some form of exercise or activities for it so that it can burn calories.

Fatty meal worms or even some type of dog good fed in wrong proportions will make your monitor lizard develop a fatty liver. If you over feed them, they could become lazy, they won't move around simply because their food is delivered to them, it won't fight back like in the wild, and they don't have to hunt for it. If you can't change the enclosure, you should probably take them out for a walk around your house (with your supervision of course) or around your yard so that they will be able to walk or use up their energy.

Metabolic Bone Disease (MBD)

The metabolic bone disease is the most common diseases among reptiles in general including monitor lizards. This disease is caused by a lack in dietary calcium, improper lighting, and also imbalanced nutrition. As mentioned earlier in the feeding chapter of this book, your monitor lizard should have the right amount of calcium and vitamins through gut – loading their food. If the calcium levels are low, the body will be forced to get calcium source straight from the bones so that there will be enough energy for the body to function especially for muscle movements and metabolism. The effect, however is that the bones become weak and eventually brittle. This disease is very painful and could be cause death for your pet Savannah.

The usual signs you should look out for is bent leg bones, double elbows, stunted growth, decrease in the use of its tongue, double knees, misaligned mouth, soft or if it's grabbing its own limbs or head. If your monitor lizard gets affected with MBD it cannot be reversed but the good news is that the process of progression of the disease can be stopped. If prevented, the bones can be treated with proper medications, and it can heal over time.

Proper husbandry such as enough access to UVB lighting as well as proper nutrition can correct the calcium imbalance in the body.

Bacterial Pneumonia

Bacterial pneumonia is caused by several respiratory factors like nasal discharge, virus and other ailments associated with the nasal cavity, lungs and breathing. Pneumonia is a very subtle and a deadly disease among monitor lizards because often times, its symptoms are unnoticeable and when owners get to notice them, the disease is already advance and difficult to treat.

The most common symptom you should look out for is a nasal discharge. Nasal discharge could mean that your pet Savannah may only have problems in its lungs, which can be easily treated with antibiotics. Respiratory infections that affect the nostrils, trachea, lungs, and air sacs can mean a severe case. Pneumonia and other respiratory problems are often caused by poor husbandry because if the lizard is not housed in a preferred optimal temperature environment it can become stress, weaken the immune system, and be predispose to other viral or bacterial illnesses.

A strong immune system is needed to attack various infections like viruses, parasites, and bacteria so that it will not progress into major illnesses. Another major factor of respiratory illnesses is humidity. Nutrition is another factor; because lack of sufficient vitamins and minerals in their diet can cause serious respiratory problems. The treatment for bacterial infections and viruses that causes respiratory problems is usually antibiotics, but it only treats secondary infections, and not the root cause of the problem.

Chapter Ten: Care Sheet and Summary

Keep in mind that lots of factors are in becoming a monitor lizard breeder. You need to make sure that the snake you're getting is healthy, and the breeder it came from is reputable or responsible. Proper feeding, good husbandry, and appropriate taming/handling can ultimately make your Savannah monitor happy and strong against serious illnesses. This chapter will give you a quick summary of all the essential things you need to remember when it comes to taking care of your pet Savannah monitor.

Biological Information

Taxonomy: *Varanus exanthematicus.* They belong in Kingdom *Animalia,* Phylum *Chordata,* Class *Reptilia,* Order *Squamata,* Family *Varanidae* Genus *Varanus,* and Species *V. exanthematicus*

Country of Origin: (Sub – Saharan) Africa

Common Areas: rocky desserts, forests, woodlands

Size: 1 - 4 1/2 feet long

Weight: 60 - 7- kg; 150 pounds

Body Type and Appearance: Savannah monitors have a stout body appearance; they also have forked tongues, possess a banded tail and have bellies that come in a variety of colors. The savannah's head is mostly rectangular in shape and also flat, they have hundreds of small yet very sharp teeth and their skin is thick with keeled scales.

Color: Their colors range from gray to brown, the back part of their bodies has darkish yellow spots, and their tails have yellow or sometimes brown rings. Their tongues are blue in color like most snake species.

Defense Mechanism: When Savannah monitors are threatened by their predators they defend themselves by lashing their tails or hissing loudly to scare off the potential predator.

Lifespan: 15 - 20 years on average

Savannah Monitors as Pets

Temperament: Captive – bred savannah monitor lizards are very easy to tame and can also be trained for socialization, they also grow quite large which is perfect for handling if you really prefer bigger types of lizard species. In the wild as well as in captivity, male savannah monitors tends to be aggressive in protecting their territories against other lizards or animals.

Other pets: All reptile species for this matter are carnivorous and natural predators. Make sure that your adult savannahs are away from your younger pet Savannahs because even if they are docile pets, every other animal species is food to them including their own kin.

Major Pro: They are docile and easy to tame as well as non – venomous unlike other monitor lizards; safe around people provided that there is supervision and they are properly handled.

Major Con: Growth may be relatively hard to manage since it can get quite heavy and long; can live up to 20 years or more which means that long – term commitment is needed

Legal Requirements and Snake Licensing:

- You will not be allowed to transport monitor lizards from one country to another if you don't have an export certificate from CITES and from the country of origin as well as the CITES import certificate to the country of your destination.
- If you want to travel or transport your pet Savannah, you should have these certificates by satisfying authorities that your pet is obtained legally. If you're going to buy or sell monitor lizards from other countries, you'll need an authorization for import to make sure that they will be legally imported.
- Make sure to research thoroughly about how to bring your pet snake to another country, and the specific laws that apply depending on what part of the region or place you will stay.
- If you don't comply with the regulations of CITES, authorities has grounds to automatically confiscate your pet Savannah or you could pay a fine, and worse imprisonment.

Estimated Costs of Keeping a Savannah Monitor:

- Savannah Monitor Lizard breed: $50 - $69

- Glass Enclosure with a screen top or lid (for hatchlings): average of $99 (depending on size)

- Glass Enclosure (for adults): $250 (complete set with regulators/heaters)

- Bedding or Substrate: $6/bag

- Water Dish(for adults/large): $20 or more (depending on size/quality)

- Heaters/Misting Equipment: around $40 total or more

- Basking Lamp/UVB bulbs: $100 or more

- Heat and Water Temperature Regulator/ Gauges: $5 or more

- Hiding Spots: $5 for young Savannahs

- Temporary tank (for young Savannahs): $30 - $50 or more

- Food: $12/bag or more (depending on brand and amount/quantity)

- Laying bin: $50

How to Acquire a Savannah Monitor Lizard

Where to Purchase: Reptile Shops, Private Breeders, Reptile Shows, Rescue Centers

Characteristics of a Reputable Breeder:

- Good breeders must be knowledgeable about the breeds they raise, and should give you specific info about the breed.

- They should be able to teach you how to properly set up the enclosure, where to place it, and the right temperature/humidity levels needed.

- Good breeders will walk you through every step of the process. They are willing to answer all of your questions and if they think that you are not a good fit as an owner, they won't sell it to you.

Characteristics of a Healthy Breed: A healthy Savannah monitor lizard should not have blisters on its skin or scale injuries; another sign to watch out for is parasite infestation in its scales. The monitor lizard should readily use its tongue to smell and search its environment; must have clear and bright eyes; should have no discharge in its eyes, ears, nostrils and cloaca. Must be active and responsive; when you lift it up, you should be able to feel a sense of strength to its body.

Setting Up a Habitat for Savannah Monitors:

- Ideally, the temporary cage for a baby Savannah monitor lizard should be a 55 – gallon tank, and once it becomes an adult the cage size should at least be 6 feet in length, 3 to 4 feet in height and 4 to 6 feet in depth.
- You need to make sure that the enclosure you will buy or build is either made out of thick glass/plexiglass or thick plywood because these animals have very sharp claws that can easily rip the enclosure apart if it's made out of mesh or low quality materials.
- Don't want to buy very large materials to put inside a cage if the enclosure itself doesn't have a wide opening or somewhat hard to access. You can also opt to purchase a glass tank since it's much affordable and provides an accessible sliding doors or glass lids.

Materials Needed for Savannah Monitor Lizard Enclosure:

- Substrate
- Spag Moss/ Plants/ Branches
- Water Dishes
- Fogger/ Misting Equipment
- Hiding Spots
- UVB light
- Heaters
- Basking light bulbs

Ideal Location of Hiding Spots:

For young Savannahs: when choosing a hiding spot, you should consider the age and current size of your monitor lizard. If you acquire a baby Savannah monitor lizard, they could adapt more easily if the enclosure has more foliage and hiding areas.

For Adults: Try to purchase a hiding spot that has some opening on it so you can also provide some branches where they can bask on. You should also place it in the pool side or near the water bowl or on the cooler side of the enclosure.

Diet for Savannah Monitors

In the wild: Savannahs are carnivorous and mostly insectivores, in the wild they love to eat worms, eggs, smaller snakes, other smaller mammals, crickets, beetles, roaches and other types of insects.

In captivity: The majority of your pet's nutrition should be insects as well as thawed or frozen mice; you can also choose to supplement their food with pre – killed mice. Don't feed your lizard with a live rodent because it can harm or cause injury to your Savannah monitor and also prompt him/her to be afraid or to stop feeding. Thawed mice/rodents and small insects like crickets, roaches, mealworms, wax worms and kingworms that are gut – loaded are the safest food to feed your Savannah monitor lizard.

In the zoo: Savannah monitors that are zoo – captives are often being fed with raw and low fat turkey, eggs as well as some supplements that are mixed suitably for optimum health

Feeding Conditions: Be sure to set up and stabilize their habitat before bringing your Savannah monitor home so they can also digest and absorb food properly

Feeding Amount/Frequency:

- Baby Savannahs that are about 1 foot long should be fed with 4 fuzzy mice every 2 to 3 days.

- Juveniles around 3 feet long should be fed 1 to 4 thawed mice at least twice a week

- Adults that are more than 3 feet should be fed 2 to 3 mice, once or twice a week.

How to Dust Your Lizard's Food

- Calcium is very important to your Savannah monitor's diet as well as the vitamins that can be found in powdered supplements. You should sprinkle or dust a small amount of these powdered supplements in the feeder insect before giving them to your pet lizard.

- Use calcium twice a week, as well as calcium with D3 and a multivitamin at least once a month.

- The time wherein you should feed your insects to your monitor lizard should be no more than twelve hours from the time you gut load it.

Husbandry for Savannah Monitor Lizards

Lighting, Temperature and Humidity Guidelines:

- The warm side of the enclosure should ideally be at 85 to 90 degrees Fahrenheit; the cool side should at least be at 80 degrees while the basking area (where the heat pads/bulbs are located) should be at 100 to 120 degrees Fahrenheit. The cage humidity's basking area should be low, while the cooler area where the hiding spot is usually located should have a high percentage of humidity level.

- If the room temperature is 75 degrees and below at night, you may want to use a supplemental ceramic heater; these heaters do not provide light like halogen or UVB bulbs so you don't really have to worry turning it on at night, your monitor lizard won't be disturb because these equipment only emits the needed supplemental heat.

- To maintain your Savannah monitor's biological rhythm or natural day and night patterns just like in the wild, you should make sure that they have at least 8 to 12 daytime and nighttime hours.

Habitat Maintenance Tips:

- Regular cleaning prevents the possible transmission of diseases which can be found in the fecal matter of reptiles, and which may be transmissible to humans.
- Spot cleaning the interior of the cage should be done as often as possible – at least once a day or once every other day.
- Before doing a full cleanse of your pet's tank, you must first find a suitable temporary cage for your monitor lizard.

Handling and Hygiene

- It's important that baby Savannah monitors get used to being having regular human contact or socializing them at a young age so that they can be tamed when they grow older.

- Avoid "death grabs"; these animals in the wild have natural instincts when it comes to becoming a prey or a predator. If you handle or try to grab them directly from the top at a vertical angle, they may mistake you as a predator and this could result to potential aggression or your pet will be scared if it's still a baby.

- Slowly put your arms down so they can climb over it or grab them on their bellies underneath slowly and support their bodies using both hands and arms.

- It's better to handle them on the side of their bodies and not in front of the head or on top because that's how predators move, and they could mistake you as the enemy.

- Don't forget to support their hind legs and forelegs because they would feel safe and comfortable that way.

- You can also make them come to you by offering some food using a spoon, once they get to identify the scent they could probably grab a bite out of it, and once they do, you can slowly slide your fingers behind the food so that he'll also be familiarized with your scent and a food scent.

Grooming Your Pet

- Savannah monitors sheds which means that they can grow a new skin while their old skin eventually falls off on its own

- Your monitor won't also need nail trimming because with the right furnishings it will prevent the nails from overgrowing.

- Some keepers give their lizards a scrub on its back so you can try doing that with your Savannah but make sure you use cleaning materials that are safe and non – toxic.

- It's recommended to check your pet for parasites to avoid any kinds of illnesses later on; you should also make sure that the enclosure is clean to avoid being harbored with bacteria, and that the water in its dish are regularly replace.

Monitor Lizard Shedding Process and Tips

- Monitor lizards shed their skin but compared to snakes, they don't do it as a whole piece but as patches.

- When your Savannah lizard begins shedding, they may usually look dull and their eyelids could at a period of time look like the eyes of a bull – frog this is all natural.

- Don't ever try to peel off the skin because it will naturally shed on its own, peeling could be really painful for your pet.

- Usually, monitor lizards shed around four to six weeks, and more often if the environment has the right temperature and humidity levels.

- Once the new skin forms, it will begin to separate from the old layer, and it will eventually fall off into patches. There will be a fluid like layer between the new and old skin which will aid in the shedding process.

- If you want to create a more humid enclosure, you can mist it twice a day whenever it's time for your pet to shed or you can use fogging equipment or misting fixtures to make it automatic.

Breeding Your Savannah Monitors

Sexual Dimorphism: Savannah monitor lizard males have usually longer heads and a bit angular face than females; they also possess a relatively larger or longer body structure than the female and a more substantial tail base. Most female savannah monitors have a roundish body structure, their tail base is usually narrower and it is tapering inward.

How to Set Up the Right Breeding Conditions:

- You can either feed your pets in the morning and have a basking spot that is on for 24/7 or just keep the light on whenever you feed them.

- If you can keep a female and a male's metabolism going every day, biologically they will feel comfortable enough to breed and support life for their offspring.

- A sign that your female is ready to mate is when it gets a bit heavier because that means that the egg are developing.

- Begin feeding them 3 to 4 times a week, you have to feed your females more frequently plus make sure that you provide them with higher dosage of vitamin D3 because they will also need that in the reproduction process.

Sexual Maturity: 1 1/2 years

Incubation Period: 5 to 6 months

Clutch Size: 15 to 20 eggs on average; 40 maximum

Laying Bin/Enclosure Temperature: 80 to 88 degrees Fahrenheit

Common Diseases and Health Requirements

- Generally healthy but predispose to Intestinal Parasites, Fatty Liver Disease, Metabolic Bone Disease (MBD), Bacterial Pneumonia

Index

D

E

F

G

H

I

M

N

O

P

R

S

T

U

V

W

Y

Photo Credits

Page 1 Photo by user Lawrence Harman via Flickr.com, https://www.flickr.com/photos/lawrenceharman/13723921445/

Page 3 Photo by user The Reptilarium via Flickr.com, https://www.flickr.com/photos/thereptilarium/5642083830/

Page 9 Photo by user Via Tsuji via Flickr.com, https://www.flickr.com/photos/via/11577195896/

Page 24 Photo by user Rod Waddington via Flickr.com, https://www.flickr.com/photos/rod_waddington/15246119875/

Page 34 Photo by user Stuart Richards via Flickr.com, https://www.flickr.com/photos/left-hand/2403408263/

Page 46 Photo by user Mark Dumont via Flickr.com, https://www.flickr.com/photos/wcdumonts/5996237125/

Page 54 Photo by user Michael Thielmeier via Flickr.com, https://www.flickr.com/photos/mike587/21220669/

Page 60 Photo by user Bjoertvedt via Wikimedia Commons, https://commons.wikimedia.org/wiki/File:Varanus_exanthematicus_Savannah_Monitor_LoroParque_IMG_6864.JPG

References

"A starting point for the care of Savannah Monitors" – Savannahmonitor.net

<http://savannahmonitor.net/>

"Bosc monitor"s – ANAPSID.org

<http://www.anapsid.org/savannah.html>

"Breeding Savannah Monitors" – ReptilesMagazine.com

<http://www.reptilesmagazine.com/Reptile-Magazines/Reptiles-Magazine/February-2010/Breeding-Savannah-Monitors/>

"Caring for Pet Savannah Monitors" - The Spruce

<https://www.thespruce.com/savannah-monitors-1239214>

"Diet" – The Savannah Monitor News

<http://thesavannahmonitornews.weebly.com/diet.html>

"Savannah monitor" – AnimalSpot.net

<http://www.animalspot.net/savannah-monitor.html>

"Savannah monitor" – LLL Reptile

<https://www.lllreptile.com/articles/47-savannah-monitor/>

"Savannah monitor" – Wikipedia

<https://en.wikipedia.org/wiki/Savannah_monitor>

"Savannah Monitor Lizard (Varanus exanthematicus)" – ReptilesAlive.com

<http://www.reptilesalive.com/savannah-monitor-lizard/>

"The Savannah Monitor: The Most Misunderstood Lizard" - ReptileApartment.com

<http://reptileapartment.com/savannah-monitor-misunderstood-lizard/>

Feeding Baby
Cynthia Cherry
978-1941070000

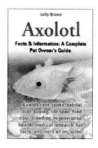

Axolotl
Lolly Brown
978-0989658430

Dysautonomia, POTS
Syndrome
Frederick Earlstein
978-0989658485

Degenerative Disc
Disease Explained
Frederick Earlstein
978-0989658485

Sinusitis, Hay Fever,
Allergic Rhinitis Explained
Frederick Earlstein
978-1941070024

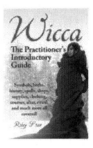

Wicca
Riley Star
978-1941070130

Zombie Apocalypse
Rex Cutty
978-1941070154

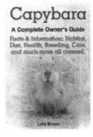

Capybara
Lolly Brown
978-1941070062

Eels As Pets
Lolly Brown
978-1941070167

Scabies and Lice Explained
Frederick Earlstein
978-1941070017

Saltwater Fish As Pets
Lolly Brown
978-0989658461

Torticollis Explained
Frederick Earlstein
978-1941070055

Kennel Cough
Lolly Brown
978-0989658409

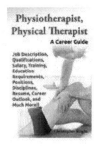

Physiotherapist, Physical
Therapist
Christopher Wright
978-0989658492

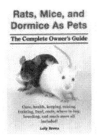

Rats, Mice, and Dormice
As Pets
Lolly Brown
978-1941070079

Wallaby and Wallaroo Care
Lolly Brown
978-1941070031

Bodybuilding Supplements
Explained
Jon Shelton
978-1941070239

Demonology
Riley Star
978-19401070314

Pigeon Racing
Lolly Brown
978-1941070307

Dwarf Hamster
Lolly Brown
978-1941070390

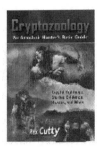

Cryptozoology
Rex Cutty
978-1941070406

Eye Strain
Frederick Earlstein
978-1941070369

Inez The Miniature Elephant
Asher Ray
978-1941070353

Vampire Apocalypse
Rex Cutty
978-1941070321

Made in the USA
Middletown, DE
09 March 2018